# The Babysitter's Handbook

The Business
of Babysitting:
*A How-To Guide*

Printed in the United States of America
by G&R Publishing Co.

Distributed By:

**CQProducts**

507 Industrial Street
Waverly, IA 50677

ISBN-13: 978-1-56383-266-6
ISBN-10: 1-56383-266-6
Item #2901

# The Babysitter's Handbook
## Table of Contents

# The Babysitter's
## Plan
*Getting Started*

# Getting Started

Babysitting is not just a pastime, it's a serious business. It's hard work and it takes a lot of responsibility to care for and keep children safe. On the other hand, it's also a lot of fun and a great way to earn some extra money. But before you jump into babysitting you should ask yourself the following questions:

❏ Are you a good leader?

❏ Are you dependable?

❏ Are you patient and kind?

❏ Do you have a sense of humor?

❏ Are you organized and do you follow instructions well?

❏ Are you willing to give up your beautiful summer days, weekends and even some week nights?

If you put a check mark next to most of these questions, you are on the road to becoming an awesome babysitter.

There are many things to do before you start your own babysitting business and the following pages can guide you through the process. You may also want to research and register for training classes and certifications available in your area. Check with your area hospital, local 4-H or American Red Cross Chapter for available babysitting courses. Make sure to let clients know you have this training and/or certification because it will help in gaining their trust and confidence in you.

Proving yourself as a mature and responsible caretaker along with treating your clients with courtesy and respect can lead to a profitable babysitting business and a fun hobby!

# What Makes a Good Babysitter?

A good babysitter needs to be dependable, organized, patient, kind and so much more. Below is a complete list of characteristics and descriptions that make a great babysitter. Check it out to see how many of these characteristics you possess.

❑ **Do you love little kids?**
The best babysitters love to be around and play with little kids. If you're having fun, the kids will have fun too.

❑ **Are you confident in yourself?**
Kids can sense whether or not you're comfortable around them. A good babysitter must be confident so kids will know who is in charge.

❑ **Do you have good leadership skills?**
Once you've established that you're the one calling the shots, you must be willing to take the reins and make good decisions.

❑ **Do you have good manners?**
Being pleasant and courteous is just as important as establishing leadership. It's also important to leave your client's house the way you found it and clean up any messes you or the children have made.

❑ **Are you patient?**
Sometimes little kids don't move as fast or learn as quickly as one would expect. And sometimes they don't understand what's right and wrong and why they should or shouldn't do some things. A good babysitter must be able to reason with and teach children without losing his or her temper.

❏ **Are you knowledgeable about children?**
Babysitters should have the basic understanding of how to feed, bathe, dress, diaper and play with younger children, and know how to care for older children as well. Taking a babysitting class through your local hospital, 4-H or American Red Cross Chapter is highly recommended.

❏ **Are you flexible?**
You should be able to adjust to different families' patterns and routines. If you are uncomfortable with the way a family does something, you should speak to them about it or decline the opportunity to work for them.

❏ **Are you aware of potential dangers?**
You should be alert to potential dangers in your surroundings. It's your job to keep the children safe.

If you haven't put a check mark next to all the characteristics above, it doesn't mean you can't be a good babysitter. If you have the desire and are willing to learn, some of these important traits can be gained with experience. You should reevaluate your abilities every few months to see what you've learned.

Below is a list of other special skills that might help you be an even better babysitter. Some of these skills are good for taking care of kids as well as entertaining them.

❏ I like to paint pictures and draw.

❏ I like to do crafts and make things with my hands.

❏ I like to sing songs.

❏ I can play a musical instrument.

❏ I like to tell stories and read books out loud.

❑ I like to act out plays and skits.

❑ I like to play dress-up.

❑ I'm in good shape. I can run, jump and play sports.

❑ I can cook.

❑ I can clean and do laundry.

❑ I'm never bored; I can always find something to do.

❑ I like to tell jokes.

❑ I can perform magic and card tricks.

❑ I can juggle.

❑ List any other skills you may have that are not listed above: _____
_____
_____
_____

**My Thoughts and Ideas:**

# *Getting the Green!*
## Making Financial Arrangements

It is important to discuss your fee in advance with all of your clients. You should tell them your rate at the time of scheduling. If you are not sure what a fair rate of pay is, check with others who babysit in your area. You can also ask your clients what they paid their last babysitter or discuss the matter with your own parents.

You should let your clients know if you prefer payment by check or cash and if you want payment at the beginning or end of your service.

When it comes time for clients to pay you, they may ask, "How much do I owe you?" You should be prepared to answer the exact amount that was discussed when you were scheduled for the job. Or say, "That is ____ hours at $____ an hour. The total is $____."

Here are some other things to think about:

- Do you charge by the hour or by the day?

- Will you charge the same for every family?

- Will you charge more for families with more children?

    Rate for 1 child: _____

    Rate for 2 children: _____

    Rate for 3 children: _____

    Rate for 4/plus children: _____

- If you are not comfortable babysitting for 4 or more children, you might want to consider limiting your service to the number of children you feel you can adequately care for by yourself.

# Client's Expectations

Before you begin a babysitting session, you should clarify the client's expectations of you. Below are some questions to ask both yourself and your client.

• What time should I arrive?

• What time will I be finished?

• Will I be required to prepare a meal or have arrangements already been made?

• Do I need to give the child a bath and put him/her to bed, or will the parents be home in time to do it themselves?
  *Never give a child a bath unless the parents ask you to do so. Because of the risk of drowning, it can be dangerous with small children. If a parent requests that you give a child a bath and you don't feel comfortable doing so, just tell them. They will more than likely understand and appreciate your honesty. You should never leave an unattended child in or near water.

• How should I handle a misbehaving child?

• Will I be required to complete extra tasks like cleaning, laundry or doing the dishes?

• Is there any schoolwork I need to help the child complete?

• Is there a pet I need to care for as well?

• How will I be getting to and from the client's home?
  *You should not have to walk anywhere alone at night, even if it is only a short distance. If you do not feel comfortable riding in a car alone with a particular parent, it may be best to make arrangements for your own parents to take you and pick you up. Don't ever get into a vehicle with a person who has consumed alcohol.

If you feel too many extra duties have been placed upon you (other than caring for the children) or you've been given an unreasonable amount of work you didn't previously agree on, you can renegotiate your fee or politely refuse to work for that particular family again.

If you've never met a family you will be babysitting for, it's a good idea to meet them in advance. You should discuss the details of your agreement, but also get to know their children, become familiar with their surroundings and see how they interact with you.

You may need to let a client know if you are not comfortable with a situation, request or an additional task. There is nothing wrong with admitting to a client you don't know how or don't feel you can handle something. It's better to do so in advance than be overwhelmed when it comes time to babysit. Parents are sure to appreciate your honesty and will probably make arrangements for you.

Check out the Contact and Information List for more information you should request from families.


**My Thoughts and Ideas:**

# The Babysitter's Clients

## Clients

*Contacts and Information Lists*

# Contact and Information List

**Family name:**_____

| Child's Name | Age | Birthday |
|---|---|---|
| _____ | _____ | _____ |
| _____ | _____ | _____ |
| _____ | _____ | _____ |
| _____ | _____ | _____ |
| _____ | _____ | _____ |

Address: _____

City:_____ State:____ Zip: _____

Phone: _____

Mother's Name: _____

Work Phone: _____ Cell: _____

Father's Name: _____

Work Phone: _____ Cell: _____

Emergency Contact 1: _____

Relationship: _____

Phone: _____

Emergency Contact 2: _____

Relationship: _____

Phone: _____

Notes: _____

_____

_____

_____

_____

**Medical**

Medications being taken: _____

_____

Allergies: _____

_____

_____

First-aid equipment is located: _____

_____

_____

**Supplies**

Diapering supplies are located: _____

_____

_____

Extra clothes or pajamas are located: _____

_____

_____

**Snacks and Meals**

Snack time is at: _____

What to eat and where it's located:_____

_____

Breakfast/lunch/dinner time is at: _____

_____

What to eat and where it's located: _____

_____

**Sleepy-time**

Naptime: _____

   Routine: _____

Bedtime: _____

   Routine: _____

# *Contact and Information List*

**Family name:**_____

| Child's Name | Age | Birthday |
|---|---|---|
| _____ | _____ | _____ |
| _____ | _____ | _____ |
| _____ | _____ | _____ |
| _____ | _____ | _____ |
| _____ | _____ | _____ |

Address: _____

City:_____ State:____ Zip: _____

Phone: _____

Mother's Name: _____

Work Phone: _____ Cell: _____

Father's Name: _____

Work Phone: _____ Cell: _____

Emergency Contact 1: _____

Relationship: _____

Phone:  _____

Emergency Contact 2: _____

Relationship: _____

Phone: _____

Notes: _____

_____

_____

_____

_____

**Medical**

Medications being taken: _____

_____

Allergies: _____

_____

_____

First-aid equipment is located: _____

_____

_____

**Supplies**

Diapering supplies are located: _____

_____

_____

Extra clothes or pajamas are located: _____

_____

_____

**Snacks and Meals**

Snack time is at: _____

What to eat and where it's located:_____

_____

Breakfast/lunch/dinner time is at: _____

_____

What to eat and where it's located: _____

_____

**Sleepy-time**

Naptime: _____

   Routine: _____

Bedtime: _____

   Routine: _____

# *Contact and Information List*

**Family name:**_____

| Child's Name | Age | Birthday |
|---|---|---|
| _____ | _____ | _____ |
| _____ | _____ | _____ |
| _____ | _____ | _____ |
| _____ | _____ | _____ |
| _____ | _____ | _____ |

Address: _____

City:_____ State:____ Zip: _____

Phone: _____

Mother's Name: _____

Work Phone: _____ Cell: _____

Father's Name: _____

Work Phone: _____ Cell: _____

Emergency Contact 1:_____

Relationship: _____

Phone: _____

Emergency Contact 2:_____

Relationship: _____

Phone: _____

Notes: _____

_____

_____

_____

_____

**Medical**

Medications being taken: _____

_____

Allergies: _____

_____

_____

First-aid equipment is located: _____

_____

_____

**Supplies**

Diapering supplies are located: _____

_____

_____

Extra clothes or pajamas are located: _____

_____

_____

**Snacks and Meals**

Snack time is at: _____

What to eat and where it's located: _____

_____

Breakfast/lunch/dinner time is at: _____

_____

What to eat and where it's located: _____

_____

**Sleepy-time**

Naptime: _____

  Routine: _____

Bedtime: _____

  Routine: _____

# *Contact and Information List*

**Family name:**_____

| Child's Name | Age | Birthday |
|---|---|---|
| _____ | _____ | _____ |
| _____ | _____ | _____ |
| _____ | _____ | _____ |
| _____ | _____ | _____ |
| _____ | _____ | _____ |

Address: _____

City:_____ State:____ Zip: _____

Phone: _____

Mother's Name: _____

Work Phone: _____ Cell: _____

Father's Name: _____

Work Phone: _____ Cell: _____

Emergency Contact 1: _____

Relationship: _____

Phone: _____

Emergency Contact 2: _____

Relationship: _____

Phone: _____

Notes: _____

_____

_____

_____

_____

**Medical**

Medications being taken: _____
_____

Allergies: _____
_____
_____

First-aid equipment is located: _____
_____
_____

**Supplies**

Diapering supplies are located: _____
_____
_____

Extra clothes or pajamas are located: _____
_____
_____

**Snacks and Meals**

Snack time is at: _____
What to eat and where it's located:_____
_____

Breakfast/lunch/dinner time is at: _____
_____

What to eat and where it's located: _____
_____

**Sleepy-time**

Naptime: _____
  Routine: _____
Bedtime: _____
  Routine: _____

# *Contact and Information List*

**Family name:**_____

| Child's Name | Age | Birthday |
|---|---|---|
| _____ | _____ | _____ |
| _____ | _____ | _____ |
| _____ | _____ | _____ |
| _____ | _____ | _____ |
| _____ | _____ | _____ |

Address: _____

City:_____ State:____ Zip: _____

Phone: _____

Mother's Name: _____

Work Phone: _____ Cell: _____

Father's Name: _____

Work Phone: _____ Cell: _____

Emergency Contact 1: _____

Relationship: _____

Phone: _____

Emergency Contact 2: _____

Relationship: _____

Phone: _____

Notes: _____

_____

_____

_____

_____

**Medical**

Medications being taken: _____

_____

Allergies: _____

_____

_____

First-aid equipment is located: _____

_____

_____

**Supplies**

Diapering supplies are located: _____

_____

_____

Extra clothes or pajamas are located: _____

_____

_____

**Snacks and Meals**

Snack time is at: _____

What to eat and where it's located:_____

_____

Breakfast/lunch/dinner time is at: _____

_____

What to eat and where it's located: _____

_____

**Sleepy-time**

Naptime: _____

   Routine: _____

Bedtime: _____

   Routine: _____

# Contact and Information List

**Family name:** _____

| Child's Name | Age | Birthday |
|---|---|---|
| _____ | _____ | _____ |
| _____ | _____ | _____ |
| _____ | _____ | _____ |
| _____ | _____ | _____ |
| _____ | _____ | _____ |

Address: _____

City: _____ State: ____ Zip: _____

Phone: _____

Mother's Name: _____

Work Phone: _____ Cell: _____

Father's Name: _____

Work Phone: _____ Cell: _____

Emergency Contact 1: _____

Relationship: _____

Phone: _____

Emergency Contact 2: _____

Relationship: _____

Phone: _____

Notes: _____

_____

_____

_____

_____

**Medical**

Medications being taken: _____
_____

Allergies: _____
_____
_____

First-aid equipment is located: _____
_____
_____

**Supplies**

Diapering supplies are located: _____
_____
_____

Extra clothes or pajamas are located: _____
_____
_____

**Snacks and Meals**

Snack time is at: _____
What to eat and where it's located: _____
_____

Breakfast/lunch/dinner time is at: _____
_____

What to eat and where it's located: _____
_____

**Sleepy-time**

Naptime: _____
  Routine: _____
Bedtime: _____
  Routine: _____

# Contact and Information List

**Family name:**_____

| Child's Name | Age | Birthday |
|---|---|---|
| _____ | _____ | _____ |
| _____ | _____ | _____ |
| _____ | _____ | _____ |
| _____ | _____ | _____ |
| _____ | _____ | _____ |

Address: _____

City:_____ State:____ Zip: _____

Phone: _____

Mother's Name: _____

Work Phone: _____ Cell: _____

Father's Name: _____

Work Phone: _____ Cell: _____

Emergency Contact 1: _____

Relationship: _____

Phone: _____

Emergency Contact 2: _____

Relationship: _____

Phone: _____

Notes: _____

_____

_____

_____

_____

**Medical**

Medications being taken: _____

_____

Allergies: _____

_____

_____

First-aid equipment is located: _____

_____

_____

**Supplies**

Diapering supplies are located: _____

_____

_____

Extra clothes or pajamas are located: _____

_____

_____

**Snacks and Meals**

Snack time is at: _____

What to eat and where it's located:_____

_____

Breakfast/lunch/dinner time is at: _____

_____

What to eat and where it's located: _____

_____

**Sleepy-time**

Naptime: _____

   Routine: _____

Bedtime: _____

   Routine: _____

# *Contact and Information List*

**Family name:**_____

| Child's Name | Age | Birthday |
|---|---|---|
| _____ | _____ | _____ |
| _____ | _____ | _____ |
| _____ | _____ | _____ |
| _____ | _____ | _____ |
| _____ | _____ | _____ |

Address: _____

City:_____ State:____ Zip: _____

Phone: _____

Mother's Name: _____

Work Phone: _____ Cell: _____

Father's Name: _____

Work Phone: _____ Cell: _____

Emergency Contact 1: _____

Relationship: _____

Phone: _____

Emergency Contact 2: _____

Relationship: _____

Phone: _____

Notes: _____

_____

_____

_____

_____

**Medical**

Medications being taken: _____

_____

Allergies: _____

_____

_____

First-aid equipment is located: _____

_____

_____

**Supplies**

Diapering supplies are located: _____

_____

_____

Extra clothes or pajamas are located: _____

_____

_____

**Snacks and Meals**

Snack time is at: _____

What to eat and where it's located: _____

_____

Breakfast/lunch/dinner time is at: _____

_____

What to eat and where it's located: _____

_____

**Sleepy-time**

Naptime: _____

  Routine: _____

Bedtime: _____

  Routine: _____

# Contact and Information List

**Family name:**_____

| Child's Name | Age | Birthday |
|---|---|---|
| _____ | _____ | _____ |
| _____ | _____ | _____ |
| _____ | _____ | _____ |
| _____ | _____ | _____ |
| _____ | _____ | _____ |

Address: _____

City:_____ State:____ Zip: _____

Phone: _____

Mother's Name: _____

Work Phone: _____ Cell: _____

Father's Name: _____

Work Phone: _____ Cell: _____

Emergency Contact 1: _____

Relationship: _____

Phone: _____

Emergency Contact 2: _____

Relationship: _____

Phone: _____

Notes: _____

_____

_____

_____

_____

**Medical**

Medications being taken: _____

_____

Allergies: _____

_____

_____

First-aid equipment is located: _____

_____

_____

**Supplies**

Diapering supplies are located: _____

_____

_____

Extra clothes or pajamas are located: _____

_____

_____

**Snacks and Meals**

Snack time is at: _____

What to eat and where it's located: _____

_____

Breakfast/lunch/dinner time is at: _____

_____

What to eat and where it's located: _____

_____

**Sleepy-time**

Naptime: _____

 Routine: _____

Bedtime: _____

 Routine: _____

# Contact and Information List

**Family name:**_____

| Child's Name | Age | Birthday |
|---|---|---|
| _____ | _____ | _____ |
| _____ | _____ | _____ |
| _____ | _____ | _____ |
| _____ | _____ | _____ |
| _____ | _____ | _____ |

Address: _____

City:_____ State:_____ Zip: _____

Phone: _____

Mother's Name: _____

Work Phone: _____ Cell: _____

Father's Name: _____

Work Phone: _____ Cell: _____

Emergency Contact 1: _____

Relationship: _____

Phone: _____

Emergency Contact 2: _____

Relationship: _____

Phone: _____

Notes: _____

_____

_____

_____

_____

**Medical**

Medications being taken: _____

_____

Allergies: _____

_____

_____

First-aid equipment is located: _____

_____

_____

**Supplies**

Diapering supplies are located: _____

_____

_____

Extra clothes or pajamas are located: _____

_____

_____

**Snacks and Meals**

Snack time is at: _____

What to eat and where it's located:_____

_____

Breakfast/lunch/dinner time is at: _____

_____

What to eat and where it's located: _____

_____

**Sleepy-time**

Naptime: _____

   Routine: _____

Bedtime: _____

   Routine: _____

# Contact and Information List

**Family name:**_____

| Child's Name | Age | Birthday |
|---|---|---|
| _____ | _____ | _____ |
| _____ | _____ | _____ |
| _____ | _____ | _____ |
| _____ | _____ | _____ |
| _____ | _____ | _____ |

Address: _____

City:_____ State:____ Zip: _____

Phone: _____

Mother's Name: _____

Work Phone: _____ Cell: _____

Father's Name: _____

Work Phone: _____ Cell: _____

Emergency Contact 1: _____

Relationship: _____

Phone: _____

Emergency Contact 2: _____

Relationship: _____

Phone: _____

Notes: _____

_____

_____

_____

_____

**Medical**

Medications being taken: _____

_____

Allergies: _____

_____

_____

First-aid equipment is located: _____

_____

_____

**Supplies**

Diapering supplies are located: _____

_____

_____

Extra clothes or pajamas are located: _____

_____

_____

**Snacks and Meals**

Snack time is at: _____

What to eat and where it's located: _____

_____

Breakfast/lunch/dinner time is at: _____

_____

What to eat and where it's located: _____

_____

**Sleepy-time**

Naptime: _____

  Routine: _____

Bedtime: _____

  Routine: _____

# *Contact and Information List*

**Family name:**_____

| Child's Name | Age | Birthday |
|---|---|---|
| _____ | _____ | _____ |
| _____ | _____ | _____ |
| _____ | _____ | _____ |
| _____ | _____ | _____ |
| _____ | _____ | _____ |

Address: _____

City:_____ State:____ Zip: _____

Phone: _____

Mother's Name: _____

Work Phone: _____ Cell: _____

Father's Name: _____

Work Phone: _____ Cell: _____

Emergency Contact 1: _____

Relationship: _____

Phone: _____

Emergency Contact 2: _____

Relationship: _____

Phone: _____

Notes: _____

_____

_____

_____

_____

**Medical**

Medications being taken: _____

_____

Allergies: _____

_____

_____

First-aid equipment is located: _____

_____

_____

**Supplies**

Diapering supplies are located: _____

_____

_____

Extra clothes or pajamas are located: _____

_____

_____

**Snacks and Meals**

Snack time is at: _____

What to eat and where it's located: _____

_____

Breakfast/lunch/dinner time is at: _____

_____

What to eat and where it's located: _____

_____

**Sleepy-time**

Naptime: _____

  Routine: _____

Bedtime: _____

  Routine: _____

# *Other Information to Request*

- Medical insurance information in case of an emergency.

- Additional phone numbers, pager numbers and contact information.

- Phone number and address of where parents will be while you are babysitting.

- Directions on how to work any appliances, baby swings, booster seats or high chairs.

- The location of the cleaning supplies.

- Any items or parts of the house that are off-limits to you and the children. Any other house rules you should know.

- Any particular television shows or channels the child is not permitted to watch.

- Are you allowed to make phone calls in moderation?

- Are you allowed to use the computer?

- The location of indoor and outdoor toys.

**My Thoughts and Ideas:**

# The Babysitter's Business
## Business
*Finding and Keeping Clients*

# *Finding and Keeping Clients*

Though you may have started babysitting for your younger siblings or cousins, there are other families in need of your help, too!

A good list of clients will help keep your babysitting business going and growing. If you're good at what you do, clients will come looking for you after a while. But, when you're first getting started, you might need to do a little extra work in order to find new families.

There are many safe and inexpensive ways to let people know you are available for babysitting. In the following section are several tips on finding new clients and keeping your current ones. At the end of this section are fill-in-the-blank, cut-out business cards. Make sure to give one to all your current clients and distribute them to possible new clients.

Make it easy for people to contact you by listing your telephone and cell phone numbers or even an e-mail address. If you don't have some of these things, ask permission to list your parents'. It's also a great idea to list a reference. A reference is someone you have worked for previously and who liked you. Ask your current clients if they are willing to be a reference for you and give their name and phone number to potential families. Remember, you should ask permission from a potential reference before using their name.

Sometimes you may lose clients because they are moving or children in the family have grown up. That's why you should continually look for new clients by advertising your services. Similar to finding new clients, you need to remind current clients of your service.

When you do decide to advertise in your community, your own safety should be a priority. Never post your contact information in public because it may fall into the wrong hands. Sit down and discuss all the possible ways to advertise with your parents and choose the ones that are the most beneficial and comfortable for you.

# Finding New Clients

Below are some tips for finding new families to offer your babysitting services. Again, discuss these ideas with your parents first to make sure they are options with which you are both comfortable.

• Put a notice in your church bulletin.

• Volunteer in your church's nursery and ask permission to hand out business cards or fliers with your contact information.

• Ask the current families you babysit for to recommend you to their friends or family. If they are willing, provide them with business cards to hand out.

• Your friends might need a break! If you have any friends with younger siblings or cousins they babysit a lot, offer your services to them as well. Let friends know you are willing to substitute for them if needed.

• Ask your mom or dad to recommend you to co-workers with small children. Provide them with business cards to hand out.

• With your parents' permission, visit the neighbors on your street who have small children. If you choose to go door-to-door in your neighborhood, you should only visit the homes of people you know. Or ask your parents to come with you.

Remember, you should never go to a stranger's home by yourself. If you are hired to babysit for a family that neither you nor your parents have ever met, it would be best to schedule a few meetings with your parents present before your first babysitting session.

If you find you are not comfortable offering your services to a family, there is nothing wrong with politely declining to work for them.

# *Keeping Current Clients*

Your business would be nothing without the people who already know and love your service. And yet, there is some competition out there, so you may have to remind them that you're there if they need you. Check out the list of ideas below on how to keep your current clients.

- After you've completed a babysitting job, send the family a thank-you note. Tell them how much fun you had, and ask them to remember you the next time they are looking for a sitter.

- Find out the dates of the children's birthdays and send a card.

- Send the entire family a holiday card. You don't have to reserve this idea for winter holidays only. Send the children Valentines, leave a May Day basket or send the family a card on St. Patrick's Day or the Fourth of July.

- Purchase small, inexpensive gift items like coloring books, crayons or puzzle books to take with you during a babysitting session for entertainment and as gifts to leave behind. Make sure to put a "to" and "from" label so parents can identify where the gifts came from. Not only is it a thoughtful gesture, but the family will think of you every time these items are used.

**My Thoughts and Ideas:**

## The Best Sitter in Your City

_____

Babysitter's Name                          Age

Phone Number:_____

Cell Phone: _____

E-mail: _____

Address: _____


## The Best Sitter in Your City

_____

Babysitter's Name                          Age

Phone Number:_____

Cell Phone: _____

E-mail: _____

Address: _____


## The Best Sitter in Your City

_____

Babysitter's Name                          Age

Phone Number:_____

Cell Phone: _____

E-mail: _____

Address: _____

## About My Service

Average Fee: _____
*Prices subject to change.*

Ages I've worked with *(check those that apply)*:

❏ Infant ❏ Toddler ❏ 4 and up ❏ 8 and up ❏ All

Reference Name: _____
Reference Phone Number: _____

- - - - - - - - - - - -

## About My Service

Average Fee: _____
*Prices subject to change.*

Ages I've worked with *(check those that apply)*:

❏ Infant ❏ Toddler ❏ 4 and up ❏ 8 and up ❏ All

Reference Name: _____
Reference Phone Number: _____

- - - - - - - - - - - -

## About My Service

Average Fee: _____
*Prices subject to change.*

Ages I've worked with *(check those that apply)*:

❏ Infant ❏ Toddler ❏ 4 and up ❏ 8 and up ❏ All

Reference Name: _____
Reference Phone Number: _____

## The Best Sitter in Your City

_____

Babysitter's Name               Age

Phone Number:_____

Cell Phone: _____

E-mail: _____

Address: _____

---

## The Best Sitter in Your City

_____

Babysitter's Name               Age

Phone Number:_____

Cell Phone: _____

E-mail: _____

Address: _____

---

## The Best Sitter in Your City

_____

Babysitter's Name               Age

Phone Number:_____

Cell Phone: _____

E-mail: _____

Address: _____

## About My Service

Average Fee: _____
*Prices subject to change.*

**Ages I've worked with** *(check those that apply)*:
❑ Infant ❑ Toddler ❑ 4 and up ❑ 8 and up ❑ All

Reference Name: _____
Reference Phone Number:_____

---

## About My Service

Average Fee: _____
*Prices subject to change.*

**Ages I've worked with** *(check those that apply)*:
❑ Infant ❑ Toddler ❑ 4 and up ❑ 8 and up ❑ All

Reference Name: _____
Reference Phone Number:_____

---

## About My Service

Average Fee: _____
*Prices subject to change.*

**Ages I've worked with** *(check those that apply)*:
❑ Infant ❑ Toddler ❑ 4 and up ❑ 8 and up ❑ All

Reference Name: _____
Reference Phone Number:_____

## The Best Sitter in Your City

_____

Babysitter's Name                              Age

Phone Number:_____

Cell Phone: _____

E-mail: _____

Address: _____


## The Best Sitter in Your City

_____

Babysitter's Name                              Age

Phone Number:_____

Cell Phone: _____

E-mail: _____

Address: _____


## The Best Sitter in Your City

_____

Babysitter's Name                              Age

Phone Number:_____

Cell Phone: _____

E-mail: _____

Address: _____

## About My Service

Average Fee: _____
*\* Prices subject to change.*

Ages I've worked with *(check those that apply)*:
❏ Infant  ❏ Toddler  ❏ 4 and up  ❏ 8 and up  ❏ All

Reference Name: _____
Reference Phone Number:_____

---

## About My Service

Average Fee: _____
*\* Prices subject to change.*

Ages I've worked with *(check those that apply)*:
❏ Infant  ❏ Toddler  ❏ 4 and up  ❏ 8 and up  ❏ All

Reference Name: _____
Reference Phone Number:_____

---

## About My Service

Average Fee: _____
*\* Prices subject to change.*

Ages I've worked with *(check those that apply)*:
❏ Infant  ❏ Toddler  ❏ 4 and up  ❏ 8 and up  ❏ All

Reference Name: _____
Reference Phone Number:_____

## The Best Sitter in Your City

Babysitter's Name _____ Age

Phone Number: _____

Cell Phone: _____

E-mail: _____

Address: _____

## The Best Sitter in Your City

Babysitter's Name _____ Age

Phone Number: _____

Cell Phone: _____

E-mail: _____

Address: _____

## The Best Sitter in Your City

Babysitter's Name _____ Age

Phone Number: _____

Cell Phone: _____

E-mail: _____

Address: _____

## About My Service

Average Fee: _____
*\* Prices subject to change.*

**Ages I've worked with** *(check those that apply)*:
❑ Infant  ❑ Toddler  ❑ 4 and up  ❑ 8 and up  ❑ All

Reference Name: _____
Reference Phone Number:_____

---

## About My Service

Average Fee: _____
*\* Prices subject to change.*

**Ages I've worked with** *(check those that apply)*:
❑ Infant  ❑ Toddler  ❑ 4 and up  ❑ 8 and up  ❑ All

Reference Name: _____
Reference Phone Number:_____

---

## About My Service

Average Fee: _____
*\* Prices subject to change.*

**Ages I've worked with** *(check those that apply)*:
❑ Infant  ❑ Toddler  ❑ 4 and up  ❑ 8 and up  ❑ All

Reference Name: _____
Reference Phone Number:_____

# The Babysitter's
## Oath
*Caring For and Keeping Kids Safe*

# Caring For and Keeping Kids Safe

The main and most important aspect of your job as a babysitter is to take care of and ensure the safety of the children you are watching. There are many things you need to know and do other than just keeping kids entertained for a few hours. Some of the things you might be responsible for include:

- Keeping children safe and out of harm's way.

- Knowing what to do in case of an emergency.

- Knowing how to treat minor injuries like cuts and scrapes.

- Encouraging good behavior and handling bad behavior appropriately.

- Preparing and serving healthy snacks and meals.

- Changing diapers on babies and toddlers.

- Putting children to bed and down for naps.

- Reporting activities to parents upon their return.

You will become more knowledgeable about items on the list above with some experience and instructions from parents. Write down any instructions they give you and if they leave something out, just ask. If you aren't sure what to ask, refer back to pages 13 through 38.

To report daily activities to parents, use the cut-out, leave behind reports provided at the end of this section. Parents will appreciate having a detailed explanation of what happened while they were gone. Feel free to make copies of this form for further use.

It's also important to respect family differences and follow each family's instructions or routine exactly as they ask you to do.

As mentioned before, it's highly recommended that you take a babysitting course and even become certified in CPR or first aid. Contact your local hospital, American Red Cross or 4-H chapter to see if they offer any of the classes suggested.

The following sections will explain your responsibilities as a babysitter in more detail. Remember, you should never assume that something is or isn't your duty while babysitting. Make sure to get detailed instructions on the care for each child you are looking after.

**My Thoughts and Ideas:**

# Let's Eat! Feeding Hungry Little Mouths

Next to changing diapers, snack and meal time can be one of a babysitter's messiest responsibilities.

First and foremost, you should ask the parents for feeding instructions, whether you are watching an infant, toddler or school-age child. It's guaranteed that every family you babysit for will have a different meal and snack plan. Here are some questions you should ask parents about meal and snack time.

• Is there a meal or snack ready, or do I need to prepare it?

• Is the child allergic to any foods? Are there any other foods they cannot or should not eat?

• What times should meals and snacks be eaten?

• Where should meals and snacks be eaten?

• Where can I find the ingredients for meals and snacks?

• If bottle-feeding a baby is necessary, are the bottles prepared and do they need to be warmed?

• Where are the supplies to prepare the bottles?

• How often should the baby be fed?

• How often during feeding should the baby be burped?

Getting children to eat a healthy and well-balanced meal can be difficult, especially when Mommy and Daddy are not there. Children may think they can get away with eating junk food because you are in charge for the day. But, unless their parents say otherwise, you must adhere to the child's normal meal plan. Check out the following great tips for getting children to eat what's on the menu.

- **Don't lose your cool.**
  If children throw a tantrum because they don't want what's been prepared for them, stay calm. Ask parents in advance how to handle such a situation. Ask if you should prepare something different or stick with what the children have been given.

- **Have fun.**
  Find a way to make meal times fun. Take turns telling a story, a joke or singing a song while sitting around the table. Make believe you've been shipwrecked on an island and this is your first meal in days. Or count how many bites it takes to clear the plate.

- **Offer praise, not rewards.**
  You can start a bad habit if you offer a reward for an expected behavior like eating a good dinner. Don't tell the child they will get a cookie if they eat their whole meal, but do offer praise and explain why it's good for them to eat well. Say, "Awesome job eating all your dinner! Now you will grow big and strong!" Offering rewards might cause the child to believe they will receive a prize for everything you ask them to do, and that's just not the case.

- **Don't cry over spilled milk.**
  When feeding children, messes cannot be avoided, especially with babies and toddlers. While most parents understand this, that doesn't mean it's okay for kids to launch their lunch to the ceiling. If something does get spilled or dumped over, don't get angry or upset; clean it up the best you can and then report it to parents when they return.


**My Thoughts and Ideas:**

# The Dirty Work of Diapers

Thankfully, changing diapers isn't an issue if you are babysitting for school-age children. However, if you are caring for a toddler or baby you will definitely be on diaper duty.

If you've never changed a diaper before, don't worry, it's not rocket science. Ask your own parents for a diaper-changing crash course before you babysit a baby or toddler. It will take five minutes at the most and, when finished, you're sure to be an expert.

Children's diapers should be changed as soon as they are dirtied. If you can't smell anything or can't tell if they are dirty, a good rule of thumb is to check diapers every hour or two to make sure they are still dry.

Similar to other daily activities, there can be personal preferences surrounding the care and changing of a child's diaper. Before babysitting for a child in diapers, you should consider asking parents the following questions.

• Does the child wear disposable diapers or cloth diapers?

• Should the child be cleaned with disposable wipes or soap and water?

• Do any diaper creams or powders need to be applied when the child is changed?

• Where are changing supplies located?

• Where should diapers be changed? Is there a changing table or changing pad somewhere in the house?
*Never leave a child unattended on a changing table since he or she could roll off.

• Where should I dispose of dirty diapers?

Potty training is another responsibility that can come with caring for a 2- to 3-year-old child. If a parent asks you to assist in potty training a child while you are babysitting, ask for detailed instructions on how to help the child, and follow the parent's schedule.

# Sweet Dreams

Even though children may be very tired at the end of a fun-filled day of play, getting them to go to bed can still be a challenge. No matter the age of the children, you should request a sleep-time routine from parents as well as tips on what to do if children can't or won't go to sleep.

Along with following the bedtime or naptime routine given to you, some very simple steps can be taken to help put children to bed without causing a fuss.

- **Begin quiet time early.**
  Quiet time can be anything from reading stories, listening to relaxing music or watching a movie approved by parents. You should begin quieting down 30 minutes to an hour before bedtime so children become relaxed and a little drowsy. This will make it easier for them to doze off.

- **No sweets!**
  Don't allow children to eat candy or have sugary drinks too close to sleep time. Sugar can provide them with an unwanted pick-me-up, making it difficult to fall asleep.

- **Stand firm.**
  Just as in other situations, you must stand your ground. If children continue to avoid bedtime, try reasoning with them. If that doesn't work, let them know their parents will be informed of their unwillingness to cooperate.

- **Hum a little tune.**
  If you are caring for a baby that is hard to settle down, gently pat him or her on the back and hum quietly. Or, hold them in your arms while you gently rock in a rocking chair.

- **Be reassuring.**
  Some children may have fears of the dark or other bedtime anxieties. Some just may be uneasy because Mommy and Daddy aren't there. Your job is to reassure children that everything is okay, and when they wake up, their parents will be home.

  No matter what, you should do your best to have the children in bed at the time their parents ask. If it's a special occasion, some parents will allow their children to stay up with you until they return home. But, you might want to start quieting them down anyway so they don't get too cranky or worn out. Doing so will make it easier for parents to get kids to bed when they return home, and they will appreciate your help.

  **My Thoughts and Ideas:**

# Safety First

When babysitting, safety is so much more than protecting kids from a minor scrape or bruise. You have to be aware of your surroundings, possible dangers and even possible intruders.

It will help to request the following important information from parents before they leave.

- Where is the fire extinguisher located?

- What is the planned escape route in case of a fire?

- Where are the security and/or fire alarms in the house and how do they work?

- Should you answer the phone and what, if any, information should you give callers? Are children allowed to answer the phone?

Broadcasting to friends that you're babysitting is not wise. Of course, your own parents should know when and where you are babysitting, but giving out information to too many sources risks it falling into the wrong hands. You wouldn't want to let a possible intruder know that you are alone in your client's home with children.

The same goes for phone calls. If your clients ask you to answer the phone, do not tell callers that adults are not home. Instead say they are "unavailable" or "unable to come to the phone at this time". Again, you do not want anyone who might take advantage of the situation to know you are home alone with children. Some general rules to ensure safety from intruders include:

- Lock all the windows and outside doors, even during the daytime.

- Do not open the door for anyone unless you are instructed to do so by parents.

- Answer the phone only if directed to do so by the parents. Keep the information you give to callers at a minimum.

    When it comes to safety awareness, your best tool is your common sense. Think your decisions through carefully and if you can't come to a conclusion about a certain situation, call the children's parents or even call your own parents.

    Children aren't always aware of things that can harm them when playing so make sure you put an immediate stop to games that could cause injury.

    Below are a few common sense tips when it comes to keeping kids safe, both indoors and out.

- Do not let children handle sharp objects, including scissors and kitchen utensils. If you need to use such utensils put them away immediately after using them.

- When preparing snacks and meals, keep children at a safe distance from the stove, oven and other kitchen appliances.

- Do not leave children unattended while eating. You do not want to be in the other room if a child starts to choke on food.

- Do not leave playing children unattended for long periods of time. If you must step away for a moment, be brief and return as soon as possible.

- If parents haven't child-proofed the home, beware of exposed electrical outlets and cords, household chemicals within reach of children, dangling cords or strings on blinds, open staircases, small objects on display and toy pieces that could fit into a baby's mouth.

- Never leave children unattended outdoors. If you have permission from parents to leave the house, you should be with the children at all times.

- Take a first-aid or CPR class to help improve your safety awareness and ability to treat minor injuries.

Here are a few high-danger areas that are prone to accidents and possible injury. Be extra alert when children are playing with or around these areas.

• Swing sets, playground equipment or trampolines.

• Swimming pools, wading pools, hot tubs or spas.

• Exercise and weight equipment.

• Garages or areas around stationary vehicles.

• Near streets or parking lots.

Of course, in the event of an emergency you should always dial 911. Another good phone number to have on hand is your local poison control center. If you do not know that number you can always call the national poison control center at (800) 222-1222.

**My Thoughts and Ideas:**

# The Daily Report

Don't let the day's activities be a mystery to parents. Let them know about all the fun you had while babysitting their children.

The following pages are filled with two-sided leave-behind reports for parents. Feel free to photocopy extra pages to use when you are babysitting or create your own report page and make copies.

Your clients will appreciate knowing if their kids ate a good dinner, took a long nap and how the time was spent while they were gone. Don't limit your report to the sections provided; use the extra space to elaborate on things that you think parents might need to know, like if someone scraped a knee, was fussy at naptime or learned a new word or skill. It's also a good way to show clients how organized you are and that you completed the tasks they requested.

**My Thoughts and Ideas:**

# *Daily Report*

**Date:** _____

**Sitter Arrival Time:** _____ **Departure Time:** _____

## Meals and Snacks

In the spaces below, list what time children ate and what they had for each snack or meal.

| Child's Name | Snack/Time | Breakfast | Lunch | Dinner |
|---|---|---|---|---|
|  |  |  |  |  |
|  |  |  |  |  |
|  |  |  |  |  |
|  |  |  |  |  |

Notes: _____

_____

_____

## Diaper Changes

❏ Information not applicable (check here)

Child: _____Time: _____ ❏ Dry ❏ Wet ❏ Dirty

Child: _____Time: _____ ❏ Dry ❏ Wet ❏ Dirty

Child: _____Time: _____ ❏ Dry ❏ Wet ❏ Dirty

Child: _____Time: _____ ❏ Dry ❏ Wet ❏ Dirty

Child: _____Time: _____ ❏ Dry ❏ Wet ❏ Dirty

Child: _____Time: _____ ❏ Dry ❏ Wet ❏ Dirty

Child: _____Time: _____ ❏ Dry ❏ Wet ❏ Dirty

Child: _____Time: _____ ❏ Dry ❏ Wet ❏ Dirty

## Naptime/Bedtime

| Child's Name | Naptime | Length of Nap | Bedtime |
|---|---|---|---|
|  |  |  |  |
|  |  |  |  |
|  |  |  |  |
|  |  |  |  |

Notes: _____
_____
_____

## Playtime

In the morning we: _____
_____
_____

In the afternoon we: _____
_____
_____

In the evening we: _____
_____
_____

## Other

Anything special or unusual that happened while you
were gone: _____
_____

# *Daily Report*

**Date:** _____

**Sitter Arrival Time:** _____ **Departure Time:** _____

**Meals and Snacks**

In the spaces below, list what time children ate and what they had for each snack or meal.

| Child's Name | Snack/Time | Breakfast | Lunch | Dinner |
|---|---|---|---|---|
|  |  |  |  |  |
|  |  |  |  |  |
|  |  |  |  |  |
|  |  |  |  |  |

Notes: _____

_____

_____

**Diaper Changes**

❑ Information not applicable (check here)

Child: _____Time: _____ ❑ Dry ❑ Wet ❑ Dirty

Child: _____Time: _____ ❑ Dry ❑ Wet ❑ Dirty

Child: _____Time: _____ ❑ Dry ❑ Wet ❑ Dirty

Child: _____Time: _____ ❑ Dry ❑ Wet ❑ Dirty

Child: _____Time: _____ ❑ Dry ❑ Wet ❑ Dirty

Child: _____Time: _____ ❑ Dry ❑ Wet ❑ Dirty

Child: _____Time: _____ ❑ Dry ❑ Wet ❑ Dirty

Child: _____Time: _____ ❑ Dry ❑ Wet ❑ Dirty

**Naptime/Bedtime**

| Child's Name | Naptime | Length of Nap | Bedtime |
|---|---|---|---|
|  |  |  |  |
|  |  |  |  |
|  |  |  |  |
|  |  |  |  |

Notes: _____

_____

_____

**Playtime**

In the morning we: _____

_____

_____

In the afternoon we: _____

_____

_____

In the evening we: _____

_____

_____

**Other**

Anything special or unusual that happened while you were gone: _____

_____

# *Daily Report*

**Date:** _____

**Sitter Arrival Time:** _____ **Departure Time:** _____

**Meals and Snacks**

In the spaces below, list what time children ate and what they had for each snack or meal.

| Child's Name | Snack/Time | Breakfast | Lunch | Dinner |
|---|---|---|---|---|
|  |  |  |  |  |
|  |  |  |  |  |
|  |  |  |  |  |
|  |  |  |  |  |

Notes: _____

_____

_____

**Diaper Changes**

❏ Information not applicable (check here)

Child: _____Time: _____ ❏ Dry ❏ Wet ❏ Dirty

Child: _____Time: _____ ❏ Dry ❏ Wet ❏ Dirty

Child: _____Time: _____ ❏ Dry ❏ Wet ❏ Dirty

Child: _____Time: _____ ❏ Dry ❏ Wet ❏ Dirty

Child: _____Time: _____ ❏ Dry ❏ Wet ❏ Dirty

Child: _____Time: _____ ❏ Dry ❏ Wet ❏ Dirty

Child: _____Time: _____ ❏ Dry ❏ Wet ❏ Dirty

Child: _____Time: _____ ❏ Dry ❏ Wet ❏ Dirty

## Naptime/Bedtime

| Child's Name | Naptime | Length of Nap | Bedtime |
| --- | --- | --- | --- |
|  |  |  |  |
|  |  |  |  |
|  |  |  |  |
|  |  |  |  |

Notes: _____

_____

_____

## Playtime

In the morning we: _____

_____

_____

In the afternoon we: _____

_____

_____

In the evening we: _____

_____

_____

## Other

Anything special or unusual that happened while you

were gone: _____

_____

# *Daily Report*

**Date:** _____

**Sitter Arrival Time:** _____ **Departure Time:** _____

**Meals and Snacks**

In the spaces below, list what time children ate and what they had for each snack or meal.

| Child's Name | Snack/Time | Breakfast | Lunch | Dinner |
|---|---|---|---|---|
|  |  |  |  |  |
|  |  |  |  |  |
|  |  |  |  |  |
|  |  |  |  |  |

Notes: _____

_____

_____

**Diaper Changes**

❑ Information not applicable (check here)

Child: _____Time: _____ ❑ Dry ❑ Wet ❑ Dirty

Child: _____Time: _____ ❑ Dry ❑ Wet ❑ Dirty

Child: _____Time: _____ ❑ Dry ❑ Wet ❑ Dirty

Child: _____Time: _____ ❑ Dry ❑ Wet ❑ Dirty

Child: _____Time: _____ ❑ Dry ❑ Wet ❑ Dirty

Child: _____Time: _____ ❑ Dry ❑ Wet ❑ Dirty

Child: _____Time: _____ ❑ Dry ❑ Wet ❑ Dirty

Child: _____Time: _____ ❑ Dry ❑ Wet ❑ Dirty

**Naptime/Bedtime**

| Child's Name | Naptime | Length of Nap | Bedtime |
|---|---|---|---|
| | | | |
| | | | |
| | | | |
| | | | |

Notes: _____

_____

_____

**Playtime**

In the morning we: _____

_____

In the afternoon we: _____

_____

_____

In the evening we: _____

_____

_____

**Other**

Anything special or unusual that happened while you

were gone: _____

_____

# *Daily Report*

**Date:** _____

**Sitter Arrival Time:** _____ **Departure Time:** _____

## Meals and Snacks

In the spaces below, list what time children ate and what they had for each snack or meal.

| Child's Name | Snack/Time | Breakfast | Lunch | Dinner |
|---|---|---|---|---|
| | | | | |
| | | | | |
| | | | | |
| | | | | |

Notes: _____

_____

_____

## Diaper Changes

❏ Information not applicable (check here)

Child: _____Time: _____ ❏ Dry ❏ Wet ❏ Dirty
Child: _____Time: _____ ❏ Dry ❏ Wet ❏ Dirty
Child: _____Time: _____ ❏ Dry ❏ Wet ❏ Dirty
Child: _____Time: _____ ❏ Dry ❏ Wet ❏ Dirty
Child: _____Time: _____ ❏ Dry ❏ Wet ❏ Dirty
Child: _____Time: _____ ❏ Dry ❏ Wet ❏ Dirty
Child: _____Time: _____ ❏ Dry ❏ Wet ❏ Dirty
Child: _____Time: _____ ❏ Dry ❏ Wet ❏ Dirty

## Naptime/Bedtime

| Child's Name | Naptime | Length of Nap | Bedtime |
|---|---|---|---|
|  |  |  |  |
|  |  |  |  |
|  |  |  |  |
|  |  |  |  |

Notes: _____

_____

_____

## Playtime

In the morning we: _____

_____

_____

In the afternoon we: _____

_____

_____

In the evening we: _____

_____

_____

## Other

Anything special or unusual that happened while you

were gone: _____

_____

# The Babysitter's Activities

## Games and Other Fun Things

# Games and Other Fun Things

Playing games with the children you are caring for can be so much fun. But sometimes it can be hard to find a good variety of things to do around the house.

Babysitting is easier on everyone if the time passes quickly and the kids are entertained, so you may want to come with a plan or schedule of things to do. It never hurts to bring your own supplies since you don't really know what your clients will have available. Pack some crayons, coloring books, glue, blunt-edge scissors, construction paper and other fun supplies, toys or games.

Some babysitters tend to get in the habit of watching television, but there are so many other cool activities you can do to pass the time. The following section is full of indoor and outdoor activities, crafts, recipes and games for you to use.

Before you plan a schedule for the day, get permission from parents for any activities you'd like to do and make sure they are appropriate for the ages of kids you are watching. Check if your clients have the supplies you need and, if not, make arrangements to get them.

Remember, it is very important that you supervise children during any and all crafts, games and activities to prevent accident or injury. Kids should never be left unattended when at play.

# *Rainy Days*
## Indoor Games and Crafts

### What or Who Am I?

**Ages:** 7 and up

**Supplies:**
Sticky notes
Marker, pen or pencil

**Directions:**
Using the marker, pen or pencil, write the name of a different animal on each sticky note. Without each player or child seeing what's on it, stick the note to his or her forehead. Sit in a circle; if there are only two of you, sit across from each other. Players take turns asking one yes or no question to try and guess the animal on his or her own head. Like: "Do I have four legs?" or "Do I have fur?" The first person to guess the animal on their own note is the winner.

**Tips:** The game can be repeated with different categories other than animals, like furniture, silverware and other everyday objects. The game can also be more complicated for older children using categories like movie stars and professional athletes.

**My Thoughts and Ideas:**

**My clients who would appreciate this activity:**

# Whose Shoes are Whose?

**Ages:** 5 and up

**Supplies:**
1 pair of shoes per player

**Directions:**
Each player should remove his or her shoes and put them in a pile in the middle of the room. Players stand back from the pile about 10 feet and at the signal, race to find their own pair of shoes. The first player to locate his or her shoes and put them on (including tying any laces) is the winner.

**Tips:** You can complicate the game by adding more shoes (other than those of the players) or adding everyone's socks to the pile. The game also can be played with hats and mittens instead of shoes and socks.

**My Thoughts and Ideas:**

**My clients who would appreciate this activity:**

# Fanning the Fish

**Ages:** 2 and up

**Supplies:**
1 piece of tissue paper per player
1 rolled up newspaper per player

**Directions:**
Cut each piece of tissue paper into the shape of a fish. Be creative! Cut the tissue paper into any size or shape of a fish you want. Through the process of elimination, players can find out what kind of tissue paper-fish works best. Roll up the newspaper. Players must fan their fish across the room using the rolled-up newspaper without touching the fish; only the air from the waving newspaper can move the fish. The first player to fan their fish across the room is the winner.

**Tip:** To make the game more difficult for older children, try setting up a simple obstacle course. For instance: players have to fan the fish down the hallway, around the chair and back down the hallway again.

**My Thoughts and Ideas:**

**My clients who would appreciate this activity:**

# Hotter, Colder

**Ages:** 4 and up

**Supplies:**
1 household object

**Directions:**
One person chooses an object to hide somewhere in the room. Other players should not see where the object is hidden. As players move around the room trying to find the object, the leader tells them they are "hotter" when they are close to the object or "colder" when they are farther away. If players are very close, the leader can say "burning" or "on fire". If they are very far away from the object, the leader can say players are "freezing" or "cold as ice". The game is won when the hidden object is found.

**My Thoughts and Ideas:**

**My clients who would appreciate this activity:**

# Huff and Puff Soccer

**Ages:** 4 and up

**Supplies:**
1 table
4 books
1 Ping Pong ball
1 drinking straw per player

**Directions:**
At both ends of the table, set up two books to make goal posts. Using a straw to blow the ball, two players or two teams of players try to score goals like in the regular game of soccer.

**My Thoughts and Ideas:**

**My clients who would appreciate this activity:**

# Sock Wrestling

**Ages:** 4 and up

**Supplies:**
1 pair of socks per player
Several pillows

**Directions:**
Using the pillows, make a circle on the floor to serve as a makeshift wrestling ring. The object of the game is for a player, using only his or her feet, to remove their opponent's socks first, without losing their own socks and while staying inside the ring.

**Tips:** To add silliness to the game, make up professional wrestling names for each player, like, "Mad Dog Matt" or "Beth the Body Crusher". One person could serve as the ring announcer and, using a pretend microphone, interview each player before and after the match.

**My Thoughts and Ideas:**

**My clients who would appreciate this activity:**

# Why? Why? Why?

**Ages:** 8 and up

**Supplies:**
1 sheet of paper per person
1 pen or pencil per person

**Directions:**
Each person writes down a question that begins with "why". For example, "Why do cats purr?" Fold the question over so it can't be seen and pass the paper to the next person or trade papers with another player. Without looking at the question, write an answer on the paper starting with "because". For example, "Because my feet stink." Then unfold and read the question and answer on each paper out loud. This game is really goofy and fun!

**Tip:** If younger children want to participate but cannot read or write yet, partner them with someone who can write, or write their questions and answers for them.

**My Thoughts and Ideas:**

**My clients who would appreciate this activity:**

# What's in a Name?

**Ages:** 8 and up

**Supplies:**
1 sheet of paper per person
1 pen or pencil per person

**Directions:**
Try to write down a complete sentence using words that start with each letter in your name. For example, the name Jane could make this sentence, **"J**ane **A**lways **N**aps **E**arly." Try making as many sentences as you can from one name, then move on to a friend or family member's name.

**My Thoughts and Ideas:**

**My clients who would appreciate this activity:**

# You're a Poet. Did You Know It?

**Ages:** 5 and up

**Supplies:**
1 sheet of paper per person
1 pen or pencil per person

**Directions:**
Choose 3 or 4 words that rhyme or sound alike. Make a poem by writing a sentence that ends with each of the rhyming words. For example, using the words hat, bat, mat and cat, the following poem was made.

Jenny put on a hat.
She picked up her bat.
She tripped on a mat,
And landed on her cat.

Sometimes the sentences won't make any sense once put together, but it's fun to see what silly and interesting combinations you can come up with.

**Tip:** Younger children can participate, too. Let them think of the words and sentences and then write the poems down for them.


**My Thoughts and Ideas:**




**My clients who would appreciate this activity:**

# Ring Toss

**Ages:** 4 and up

**Supplies:**
1 (4-legged) stool
4 paper plates

**Directions:**
Turn the stool upside down. Cut the center out of the paper plates to make rings. Designate a certain number of points for each leg on the stool. For instance, the front right leg is worth 1 point, the front left leg is worth 2 points, the back right leg is worth 3 points and the back left leg is worth 4 points. Players take turns trying to toss the 4 rings. The person who racks up the most points from landing rings on the legs of the stool wins the game.

**Tip:** To make the game more of a challenge, ask older players to stand farther away from the stool than younger players.

**My Thoughts and Ideas:**

**My clients who would appreciate this activity:**

# Easy as Counting to Eight

**Ages:** 8 and up

**Supplies:**
A radio and your favorite song

**Directions:**
Did you know that choreographed dances are made up by counting to eight over and over? Pick your favorite song and play it on the raidio. Find the beat and start clapping. The beat usually happens on an even count. So count 1, clap on 2 , count 3, clap on 4, count 5, clap on 6, count 7 and clap on 8. When you've found the beat and the counts, make up a move or step to each count. Put all the counts and moves together and you've made up a dance step! You can continue to repeat your 8-count to the music, or make up another 8-count and add the two 8-counts together to make a complete section of a dance. Keep adding 8-counts to make up an entire dance.

**My Thoughts and Ideas:**

**My clients who would appreciate this activity:**

# This AND That

**Ages:** 4 and up

**Directions:**
The object of the game is to finish a phrase or group of words that commonly have "and" in between. The game leader will say, "peanut butter and ..." and players will then try to be the first to finish the phrase. Each finished phrase equals 1 point. The first person to earn 5 points is the winner. After each round, the game leader can rotate.

**Tip:** Phrases can become more difficult as players become older. Younger children can answer questions like "macaroni and cheese," "bread and butter," or "hugs and kisses". Older children can answer questions like," Romeo and Juliet" or "David and Goliath".

**My Thoughts and Ideas:**

**My clients who would appreciate this activity:**

# Iceberg Hopping

**Ages:** 3 and up

**Supplies:**
4 to 5 white bed pillows

**Directions:**
Space the four pillows out across the room. Pretend that players are penguins in the Arctic and the pillows are icebergs. Each player must jump from pillow to pillow. Penguins have to land, with both feet at once on each iceberg. If a player misses or lands on one foot only, they have fallen into the icy waters and must take another turn, going back to the beginning. The first penguin to make it safely to all 4 pillows wins the game.

**Tips:** To make the game more difficult, play in rounds and space pillows farther apart with each round. Or add more pillows as you go.

**My Thoughts and Ideas:**

**My clients who would appreciate this activity:**

# Funny Putty

**Ages:** 4 and up

**Supplies:**
½ C. white glue
½ C. liquid starch
3 drops food coloring, any color, optional

**Directions:**
In a shallow dish, place the white glue. Slowly add the liquid starch to the white glue, kneading it as you go. The more the mixture is kneaded the better the consistency will be. Add 3 drops of food coloring while kneading, if desired.

**Note:** Food coloring can be messy and might stain clothing. Ask permission from parents before using it. If you and the children can be fun and creative with plain white putty, it might be wise to omit food coloring with this hands-on recipe.

**My Thoughts and Ideas:**

**My clients who would appreciate this activity:**

# Handmade Glitter

**Ages:** 4 and up

**Supplies:**
½ C. salt
3 drops food coloring, any color

**Directions:**
Preheat the oven to 350°. In a small bowl, mix the salt and food coloring. Spread the mixture over a baking sheet. Bake for 10 minutes. Remove from baking sheet and let cool completely before using the glitter to create artwork.

**My Thoughts and Ideas:**

**My clients who would appreciate this activity:**

**Warning:** This activity requires the use of an oven. Ask for parents' permission before using their oven, and keep young children away.

# Bean Balloons

**Supplies:**
3 plastic baggies
3 twist ties
4½ C. dried beans, divided
6 balloons

**Directions:**
Fill each plastic baggie with 1½ cups dried beans and close with a twist tie. Cut the open end of each balloon off. Stretch a balloon over one end of each bean-filled baggie covering the twist tie. Stretch another balloon over the other side so the baggie is completely covered. Use the bean balloons to juggle or play catch.

**My Thoughts and Ideas:**

**My clients who would appreciate this activity:**

# Homemade Sticker Stamps

**Ages:** 4 and up

**Supplies:**
½ C. plus 1 T. white glue
1 T. white vinegar
Pictures, clippings and cut-outs
Paintbrush

**Directions:**
In a small bowl, mix together the white glue and white vinegar. Paint the glue on any photo or piece of paper you want to use as a sticker. The glue can also be used on envelopes. Once the glue dries, children can lick or dab the stickers with a wet cloth and attach them to paper to make a creative collage or piece of artwork.

**My Thoughts and Ideas:**

**My clients who would appreciate this activity:**

# Fabulous Face Paint

**Ages:** 2 and up

**Supplies:**
1 plastic cup or bowl
½ C. plus 1 tsp. cornstarch
½ tsp. cold cream
½ tsp. water
2 drops food coloring, any color

**Directions:**
In the plastic cup or bowl, mix together the cornstarch, cold cream, water and food coloring. Make several different batches using different colors of food coloring with the recipe above. Apply to the face for artistic fun. Wash off with soap and water.

**Tips:** Repeat the above recipe with different shades of food coloring for more colors. Again, food coloring can stain clothing. Children may want to wear and old shirt or smock with this hands-on craft.

**My Thoughts and Ideas:**

**My clients who would appreciate this activity:**

# The Coolest Finger Paint

**Ages:** 4 and up

**Supplies:**
1 C. flour
1 pack unsweetened Kool-Aid, any flavor
¼ C. salt
1½ C. boiling water
1½ tsp. vegetable oil

**Directions:**
In a medium bowl, combine the flour, Kool-Aid and salt. Add the boiling water and oil to the mixture and stir well; and let cool. Dip fingers in paint to create cool art on paper.

**Tip:** Repeat the above recipe with different flavors of Kool-Aid for more colors.

**My Thoughts and Ideas:**

**My clients who would appreciate this activity:**

# Some other fun things to pass the time indoors:

- Read a book.
- Sing songs.
- Put puzzles together.
- Play board games.
- Play "Simon Says".
- Play "I Spy".
- Make silly faces at one another.
- Write a story.
- Color or paint pictures.

**My Thoughts and Ideas:**

# *Fun in the Sun*
## Games to Play Outside

## Tunnel Tag

**Ages:** 4 and up

**Directions:**
One player is declared "It" and must tag the others in the game. When someone is tagged, they must freeze and stand still with their legs shoulder-width apart. To become unfrozen, another player who is not "It" must crawl between the legs of the person that is frozen. If all players become frozen, then "It" wins the game and the person who has been frozen the longest becomes "It".

**My Thoughts and Ideas:**

**My clients who would appreciate this activity:**

# Double Take

**Ages:** 4 and up

**Supplies:**
1 sheet of paper per player
1 pen or pencil per player

**Directions:**
With permission from parents, take a walk in the neighborhood and try to notice four things you have not seen before. When you come home, make a list describing these things or draw a picture of them.

**My Thoughts and Ideas:**

**My clients who would appreciate this activity:**

# Balloon Pop

**Ages:** 4 and up

**Supplies:**
1 balloon per player
1 (2-foot) piece of string or ribbon per player

**Directions:**
Blow up the balloons and, using the string or ribbon, tie one around each player's ankle. Players must try to stomp on and pop the others' balloons while protecting his or her own. The player whose balloon has remained un-popped wins the game.

**My Thoughts and Ideas:**

**My clients who would appreciate this activity:**

# Take Flight

**Ages:** 3 and up

**Supplies:**
Paper cups
Paper plates
Paper
White glue
Blunt-edge scissors
Sidewalk chalk

**Directions:**
Turn the paper plate upside down and glue the open end of the cup to the top to make a flying saucer. Fold the paper in the shape of a paper airplane. Choose a starting point and draw a circle or landing zone about 10 feet away using sidewalk chalk. Let children hurl flying saucers like Frisbees and toss paper planes in the air trying to land them in the circle. As you experiment, modify the aircraft or create new ones that might fly better.

**Tips:** To continue the activity for a longer period of time, try launching aircraft from different starting points like the front porch, the backyard deck or the top of the slide on the swing set. Or move the landing zone farther away from the starting point.

**My Thoughts and Ideas:**

**My clients who would appreciate this activity:**

# Chasing Your Tail

**Ages:** 4 and up

**Supplies:**
1 handkerchief, bandana or towel

**Directions:**
Players stand in a single file line and link together by holding each other around the waist. The player at the end of the line hangs the handkerchief, bandana or towel out of his or her back pocket, like a tail. The players at the front of the line chase the back of the line in circles trying to catch the tail. Players in the middle of line can help the head of the line or make it more difficult, depending on their whim. If the line breaks, the person who let go must sit down and other players continue with a shorter line. If the tail is caught, the game is started over with a new head and a new tail.

**My Thoughts and Ideas:**

**My clients who would appreciate this activity:**

# Lollipop in a Leaf Pile

**Ages:** 3 and up

**Supplies:**
1 lollipop, still in the wrapping
1 rake per person
Pile of leaves

**Directions:**
Just like a needle in a haystack, it's pretty tough to find a lollipop in a leaf pile. If you're babysitting during the fall season, parents are sure to appreciate kids doing a little yard work. First rake leaves into a big pile. Have players turn around while the lollipop is hidden in the pile. At the signal, players jump into the pile and try to find the lollipop. The person who finds the lollipop is the winner and gets a sweet treat! When you are finished with the game, have a competition to see who can bag up the most leaves to clean up the mess.

**Tip:** If children are not permitted to eat sweets or are too young to have candy, put some crackers or cereal in a resealable snack bag and hide it in the pile.

**My Thoughts and Ideas:**

**My clients who would appreciate this activity:**

# Lightning Bug

**Ages:** 4 and up

**Supplies:**
1 flashlight

**Directions:**
This is a fun tag game for after dark. The chosen player or "lightning bug" is given an unlit flashlight. The "lightning bug" walks away from the other players in any direction and counts to 20. Once he or she gets to 20, the "lightning bug" flashes the light once. Other players then set out in pursuit of the "lightning bug". The "lighting bug" must continue to move around and count to 20, flashing his or her light each time the number 20 is reached. The player who catches the "lightning bug" is the winner, and then takes his or her place for the next game.

**Tips:** Make sure to ask permission from parents before taking kids out after dark. This game should be played in the confines of one's own backyard so children don't wander off too far or get lost.

**My Thoughts and Ideas:**

**My clients who would appreciate this activity:**

# Hop, Skip and Jump

**Ages:** 3 and up

**Supplies:**
3 outdoor objects or landmarks

**Directions:**
Choose three landmarks in the backyard, like a sandbox, a bush and a lawn chair. From the start line to the first landmark, players must hop on one foot. From the first to the second landmark, they must skip. From the second to the third landmark, they must jump. And from the third landmark back to the start line, they must do a combination of hopping, skipping and jumping. The first to finish and do so with the correct combination is the winner. If a player performs the wrong movement, he or she must start the race over.

**Tips:** If you have several players, separate them into teams and have a relay race. Or, make the race more difficult by adding more landmarks and more forms of movement like galloping, running or dancing.

**My Thoughts and Ideas:**

**My client who would appreciate this activity:**

# Tic-Tac-Toe Toss

**Ages:** 4 and up

**Supplies:**
Sidewalk chalk
1 penny or pebble per player

**Directions:**
Using the chalk, draw a large tic-tac-toe grid on the sidewalk, patio or driveway. The first player tries to toss a penny or pebble into one of the squares of the grid. Wherever the marker lands, the player draws an "X" with chalk. The second player does the same, marking squares with an "O". If the marker lands on a line or square that is already occupied, it is considered a missed turn. Like the normal game of tic-tac-toe, the player who places 3 of their own marks in a horizontal, vertical or diagonal row wins the game. To play a new game, draw a new grid or use water from a squirt bottle, hose or bucket to wash the existing grid off the sidewalk, patio or driveway.

**My Thoughts and Ideas:**

**My clients who would appreciate this activity:**

# Volley-Beach-Ball

**Ages:** 3 and up

**Supplies:**
2 lawn chairs
1 piece of string
1 blow-up beach ball

**Directions:**
Set up the 2 chairs across from each other and
tie the rope between them to create a makeshift net.
Similar to the game of volleyball, players bat the ball
back and forth across the net and try to make a point
by landing the beach ball on the ground on the
opposing team's side of the net. The team that
scores 15 points first wins the game.

**Tip:** To make the game easier, allow younger children
one bounce on the ground before they have to hit the
beach ball.

**My Thoughts and Ideas:**

**My clients who would appreciate this activity:**

# Backyard Maze

**Ages:** 2 and up

**Supplies:**
Lawn chairs and other outdoor furniture
Buckets
Cardboard boxes
Stopwatch, optional

**Directions:**
Set up lawn chairs, tables, buckets, cardboard boxes and anything else you can find around the yard into a maze or obstacle course. Kids will love scurrying through, crawling under and climbing over the objects.

**Tip:** To make the game more difficult for older children, time them with the stopwatch to see who can complete the maze or course the fastest.

**My Thoughts and Ideas:**

**My clients who would appreciate this activity:**

# Ring That Bell

**Ages:** 5 and up

**Supplies:**
1 blindfold, dishtowel, handkerchief
    or bandana per player
1 bell

**Directions:**
Blindfold all players but one. The one player that is not blindfolded is given a bell. He or she rings the bell while continuously moving around the yard. Without running into each other or anything in the yard, blindfolded players try to catch the bell ringer by listening to the ringing bell. Players should be reminded to take their time when moving around the yard blindfolded and hold their hands out in front of them while walking. The game is over when the bell ringer is caught. The person who catches the ringer then takes his or her place in the next game.

**Tips:** This game should be played in the confines of one's own backyard so children don't wander off too far or get lost. As a babysitter, you should not play the game, but rather supervise to avoid children being injured.

**My Thoughts and Ideas:**

**My client who would appreciate this activity:**

# Nature Collage

**Ages:** 2 and up

**Supplies:**
1 bottle white glue
1 pair of blunt-edge scissors per person
1 sheet of heavyweight paper per person

**Directions:**
Send children into the yard to collect leaves, pebbles, seeds, twigs, berries, feathers and any other natural items they can find. Cut, glue and paste the items found in the yard onto the paper to create a beautiful nature collage.

**Tips:** Help younger children search for items as well as cutting or pasting them. Make the task more difficult for older children by giving them a specific list of things to find in the yard. Turn it into a backyard scavenger hunt with the end result being the artwork created.

**My Thoughts and Ideas:**

**My clients who would appreciate this activity:**

# Brew Your Own Bubbles

**Ages:** 2 and up

**Supplies:**
1 tsp. sugar
½ C. water
¼ C. liquid dishwashing soap
1 plastic plate or pie tin
Plastic straws, plastic cups or old clothes hangers

**Directions:**
In a medium bowl, dissolve the sugar into the water.
Stir in the liquid dishwashing soap. Pour the solution
into a large flat container like a plastic plate or pie
tin. Use plastic straws to make small bubbles or old
clothes hangers to make large ones. Also, you can cut
the bottoms out of plastic cups to create medium-sized
bubbles. Dip the bubble-making object into the solution
and gently blow through it or wave it through the air to
see the bubbles fly.

**Tips:** Store the leftover bubble solution in an airtight
container for later use. When blowing bubbles
through a straw, be careful that younger children
don't get confused and suck the bubble solution into
their mouths. It is not dangerous, but it doesn't taste
very good!

**My Thoughts and Ideas:**

**My clients who would appreciate this activity:**

# Spray Bottle Chalk

**Ages:** 4 and up

**Supplies:**
4 T. cornstarch
1 C. warm water
3 drops food coloring, any color
1 plastic spray bottle

**Directions:**
In a medium bowl, mix together the cornstarch and warm water. Add 3 drops of food coloring and mix well. Pour the mixture into a spray bottle. Create art by spraying and squirting the mixture on sidewalks, driveways, snow or sand.

**My Thoughts and Ideas:**

**My clients who would appreciate this activity:**

# *Some other fun things to pass the time outdoors:*

- Walk the dog.
- Draw with sidewalk chalk.
- Run through the hose or sprinkler.
- Plant flowers.
- Play catch.
- Jump rope.
- Have a backyard picnic.
- Have a three-legged or sack race.
- Bob for apples.
- Play "Follow the Leader".
- Fly a kite.

**My Thoughts and Ideas:**

# *Let's Play Pretend*
## Baby, You're a Star

Create your own television show, movie, play or documentary.

**1.** Choose a topic, a favorite television show, nursery rhyme or fairy tale and start by writing a script.

**2.** Everyone can star in the show, but assign kids to other duties and roles as well, like hair, makeup, set design, costume design, lighting, stage manager, director and more. If you don't actually have supplies to fulfill these tasks, find anything; that's the beauty of pretending. You can pretend to put on makeup and style hair. Help younger children complete their tasks so they can participate as well.

**3.** Collect dolls and stuffed animals to serve as your studio audience.

**4.** If you have access to a video camera, record your production for parents to view when they return home.


**My Thoughts and Ideas:**



**My clients who would appreciate this activity:**

# Let's Go to the Zoo

1. Gather up all the stuffed animals you can find in the house.

2. Using boxes, chairs, tables and anything else you can find that will work, make pretend cages for each stuffed animal.

3. Using paper and pen, label each cage with the type of animal it contains. Have older children look in encyclopedias to find interesting facts about the animals to add to the label. You could also look on the Internet, but should ask permission from parents before using the computer.

4. If you don't have stuffed animals to represent all those you'd like to see in your zoo, have some children pretend to be the animals.

5. Assign someone to the role of zookeeper to pretend to feed and take care of the animals while others visit the zoo. Take turns in each role.

**My Thoughts and Ideas:**

**My clients who would appreciate this activity:**

# Let's Go Shopping

**1.** Using old boxes, paper, pencils and crayons, create food that you would find in the grocery store. If you have some play food, use that as well.

**2.** Ask children how much they think it costs and place a price tag on each item.

**3.** If you don't already have some play money, use paper, pencils, markers and crayons to make pretend money.

**4.** Use old shopping bags or baskets for children to put food in while they pretend to shop.

**5.** Assign someone to the job of stock boy or girl to replace items or make new items to replace those that have been purchased. Assign an older child to the role of cashier and add up the purchases.

**Tip:** The same game can be played as a clothing store, pet store or any other type of retail store.


**My Thoughts and Ideas:**



**My clients who would appreciate this activity:**

# The Perfect Puppet Show

1. Turn paper lunch bags upside down and draw faces and characters on the side of the bag using crayons and markers. The fold in the bag can serve as the mouth. When you slip your hand in the opening of the bag, place your fingers in the fold and move the flap up and down so it looks like the character is speaking.

2. Create backdrops and scenery on large pieces of poster board or construction paper by drawing backgrounds on them with the crayons and makers.

3. Attach the backdrop to the wall (in a way that it won't cause damage to paint or wallpaper) and pull a table in front of it so the scenery sits just above it.

4. Put a blanket or tablecloth over the table.

5. Children can sit behind the table so they won't be seen and hold their puppets up in front of the backdrop to put on a show.

**My Thoughts and Ideas:**

**My clientst who would appreciate this activity:**

# Under the Big Top

1. Find out what special talents the children have and put on a circus. Children can perform dances, card tricks, acrobatics, hoola hoop, juggle and more.

2. Use a flashlight as your spotlight and shine the light on each child as he or she performs.

3. Assign someone to be the ringmaster to introduce each performer.

4. Take turns acting as clowns between each performance.

5. Children can even pretend to be circus animals and perform tricks.

**My Thoughts and Ideas:**

**My clients who would appreciate this activity:**

# Playing Pretend With Toddlers

Playing pretend or make-believe is a great game for toddlers to develop social skills, but they may not be able to understand how to participate in the make-believe games listed. Young children love to mimic people who are older than them. Listed below are some simple ways to involve children 3 years old or younger.

- Ask children to imitate their favorite animal and the sounds they make.

- Host a pretend tea party.

- Make a pretend meal.

- Pretend to be a horse and let children ride on your back.

- Play with baby dolls, cars and other toys that encourage imagination and role play.

**My Thoughts and Ideas:**

**My Clients who would appreciate these activities:**

# What's Cookin'?

Letting kids choose and make their own healthy snack is a great way to pass the time and work up an appetite.

But before you begin any sort of activity in the kitchen involving kids, make sure you have parents' permission to do so. If parents do approve your fun kitchen activities, give them a list of ingredients you will need, or pick up a few things from the store yourself before heading over to babysit. Recipes involving sharp utensils, the oven and/or microwave should only be made with older children.

It's also a good idea to make sure the children you are babysitting for don't have any food allergies. If they do, avoid making recipes with foods they are unable to eat or come in contact with.

The following pages are full of easy recipes that let kids, with your expert assistance, be the cooks. Refer back to pages 54 and 55 for more clues on getting kids to eat.

**My Thoughts and Ideas:**

# Fruit-Picks

1 C. whole strawberries, cleaned and hulled
1 banana, peeled and sliced
1 C. seedless grapes
1 C. vanilla yogurt
Toothpicks

Arrange the strawberries, bananas, grapes on a plate with a bowl containing the yogurt in the middle. Allow children to choose different pieces of fruit to put on their toothpicks. Then dip fruit in the yogurt.

**Tips:** Children under 4 years old should not handle a toothpick. Younger children can just use their fingers or a fork to pick pieces of fruit and dip them in yogurt.

# Noah's Ark

1 stalk celery, cut into 3-inch pieces
½ C. peanut butter
½ C. animal crackers

Spread peanut butter onto each piece of celery. Allow the children to place animal crackers, standing upright, in the peanut butter.

**Tip:** The same recipe can be used for Ants on a Log. Simply replace the animal crackers with raisins.

# Perfectly Easy Pita Pizzas

1 pita
3 T. ketchup or tomato sauce
½ C. shredded Mozzarella cheese

Preheat the oven to 350°. Cut the pita into triangle-shaped segments. Top with ketchup or tomato sauce and sprinkle with cheese. Place the segments on a baking sheet. Bake in the oven for 8 minutes or until cheese is melted and bubbly.

**Tips:** To make this recipe more fun for kids, add other ingredients to the list like pepperoni, mushrooms, pineapple, peppers and more. Let children choose what to put on their own pizza. If you don't have pita bread, you can substitute with a plain bagel.

# Totally Tortilla Chips

1 flour tortilla
2 T. butter, divided

Preheat the oven to 350°. Cut the tortilla into triangle-shaped segments. Lightly grease a baking sheet with 1 tablespoon butter. Place the tortilla segments on the baking sheet and spread the remaining tablespoon of butter on the pieces. Bake in the oven for 10 to 15 minutes or until the tortilla chips are crispy and golden.

# P-B Banana Wraps

1 flour tortilla
1 T. peanut butter
1 banana, peeled and sliced
1 T. honey

Spread the peanut butter over the tortilla. Place the banana slices over the peanut butter and drizzle with honey. Roll the tortilla up and cut into slices.

# Gone Fishing

1 blue plate or blue piece of paper
½ C. Goldfish crackers
½ C. pretzel sticks
1 T. peanut butter

Spread the Goldfish crackers over the plate or paper. Dip one end of the pretzel sticks into the peanut butter. Using the end with peanut butter on it, try to pick the Goldfish crackers off the plate or paper. Kids will enjoy eating the fish and the pole!

# Orange Cow Cooler

1 C. milk
½ C. orange juice
1 C. diced banana

Pour the milk, orange juice and diced banana into a blender. Blend until smooth. To serve, pour drink into a tall glass.

# Peanut Butter Modeling Dough

½ C. creamy peanut butter
¼ C. nonfat dry milk
¼ C. powdered sugar
3 T. corn syrup

In a large bowl, combine the peanut butter, nonfat dry milk, powdered sugar and corn syrup. Mix until smooth. The dough can be used for shaping and molding or munching and eating.

# Crispy No-Bake Cookies

½ C. peanut butter
½ C. corn syrup
¼ C. orange juice concentrate
1½ C. nonfat dry milk
4 C. crispy rice cereal
1 T. powdered sugar

In a medium bowl, combine the peanut butter, corn syrup, orange juice concentrate and nonfat dry milk. Mix thoroughly. Pour the cereal into the peanut butter mixture and stir. Shape the mixture into small balls and roll in the powdered sugar. Place the cookies on a plate and refrigerate for 1 to 2 hours before serving.

# Five Cup Salad

1 C. mandarin oranges
1 C. pineapple chunks
1 C. flaked coconut
1 C. miniature marshmallows
1 C. sour cream

In a large bowl, combine mandarin oranges, pineapple, flaked coconut, miniature marshmallows and sour cream; mix well. Chill for 30 minutes in the refrigerator before serving.

# Apple Explosions

1 apple, cored
2 T. peanut butter
2 T. granola
2 T. raisins

Press the peanut butter into the empty core of the apple. Sprinkle the top of the apple with granola and raisins.

**Tip:** For an even sweeter treat, sprinkle the top with mini chocolate chips, mini marshmallows or coconut.

# Coconut Crisps

6 slices white bread, each cut into strips of 4
1 (14 oz.) can sweetened condensed milk
2⅔ C. flaked coconut

Preheat the oven to 375°. Roll the white bread strips in the condensed milk. Then roll the bread in the coconut. Place strips on a well-greased baking sheet. Bake for 8 to 10 minutes. Remove the strips from the baking sheet immediately and allow to cool before eating.

# Cinnatwists

1 T. cinnamon
1 C. sugar
1 (10.8 oz.) tube refrigerator biscuits
½ C. melted butter

Preheat oven to 350°. In a medium bowl, mix together the cinnamon and sugar. Stretch each biscuit into an oval shape. Dip both sides of each biscuit into the melted butter. Then dip biscuits into the cinnamon and sugar mixture. Twist the biscuits 3 to 4 times and place on a baking sheet. Bake for 10 to 12 minutes or until golden brown.

# Honey Rounds

⅔ C. honey
⅔ C. peanut butter
1 C. nonfat dry milk
⅔ C. flaked coconut

In a medium bowl, mix together the honey, peanut butter, nonfat dry milk and coconut. Roll the mixture into small balls and place on a baking sheet. Chill in the refrigerator for 1 to 2 hours before serving.

# Yummy Yogurt and Pears

1 medium pear, cored and diced
½ C. fruit-flavored yogurt
3 T. granola

In a small bowl, mix together the pears and yogurt.
Sprinkle the granola over top of the yogurt and serve.

# Cheesy Ham Roll-ups

1 (10 oz.) tube refrigerated crescent rolls
2 T. prepared mustard, divided
¼ C. shredded Cheddar cheese, divided
¼ C. finely chopped, fully-cooked ham

Preheat the oven to 375°. Unroll crescent rolls and tear
along the perforations. Place 4 crescent roll triangles
on an ungreased baking sheet. Spread 1/2 tablespoon
of mustard over each crescent roll. Sprinkle each with
1 tablespoon of cheese and 1 tablespoon of cooked
ham. Starting at the large end, roll the dough toward
the point. Fold ends in slightly to form "horns". Bake in
the oven for 11 to 13 minutes or until golden. Remove
from the oven and let cool before serving.

# Index

## The Babysitter's Plan
### Getting Started

## The Babysitter's Clients
### Contacts and Information Lists

## The Babysitter's Activities
### Games and Other Fun Things

## The Babysitter's Oath
### Caring For and Keeping Kids Safe

## The Babysitter's Activities
### Games and Other Fun Things

### Let's Play Pretend

### What's Cookin'